DIMENSIONS OF HEALTH

INTELLECTUAL HEALTH

by Kurt Waldendorf

FOCUS READERS.
NAVIGATOR

WWW.FOCUSREADERS.COM

Copyright © 2026 by Focus Readers®, Mendota Heights, MN 55120. All rights reserved. No part of this book may be reproduced or utilized in any form or by any means without written permission from the publisher.

Focus Readers is distributed by North Star Editions:
sales@northstareditions.com | 888-417-0195

Produced for Focus Readers by Red Line Editorial.

Photographs ©: Shutterstock Images, cover, 1, 4–5, 7, 8–9, 11, 12, 15, 20–21, 23, 26–27, 29; Red Line Editorial, 13; iStockphoto, 16–17, 19, 24

Library of Congress Cataloging-in-Publication Data
Library of Congress Cataloging-in-Publication Data is available on the Library of Congress website.

ISBN
979-8-88998-525-9 (hardcover)
979-8-88998-585-3 (ebook pdf)
979-8-88998-557-0 (hosted ebook)

Printed in the United States of America
Mankato, MN
082025

ABOUT THE AUTHOR

Kurt Waldendorf is the author of more than a dozen books for children. When he's not writing or editing, he enjoys indoor rock climbing and running along the shore of Lake Michigan with his dog. He lives in Chicago.

TABLE OF CONTENTS

CHAPTER 1
Finding Focus 5

CHAPTER 2
What Is Intellectual Health? 9

CONNECTIONS
Mind and Body 14

CHAPTER 3
Different Ways of Learning 17

CHAPTER 4
Goals and Questions 21

CHAPTER 5
Keeping an Open Mind 27

Focus Questions • 30
Glossary • 31
To Learn More • 32
Index • 32

CHAPTER 1

FINDING FOCUS

A boy stares at his computer screen. He can't focus. It's the spring of 2020. The COVID-19 **pandemic** has spread around the world. To stay safe, the boy no longer travels to school each day. Instead, he learns at home. Sometimes, he joins video calls with his class. Other times, he works on his own.

During the COVID-19 pandemic, many schools held classes online.

The changes have been hard. At home, there are more distractions. The boy has a hard time paying attention. He misses his friends, too. He starts acting out.

The boy's teacher speaks to his parents. Together, they come up with a plan. His parents make a schedule. It shows him

ADHD

The pandemic was especially hard for students with ADHD. *ADHD* stands for "attention deficit hyperactivity disorder." People with ADHD struggle with focus. Even small changes to schedules or surroundings have a big effect on them. They may get distracted. Or they may **fixate** on one thing. Learning skills for managing time can help. So can taking breaks.

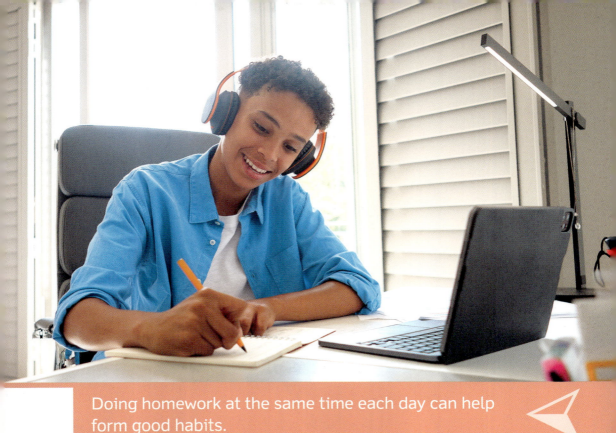

Doing homework at the same time each day can help form good habits.

when to work on each class. They also set up a desk in a quiet part of the home.

Over time, the boy's schoolwork improves. He also finds new interests. He practices drawing. The pandemic is still hard to deal with. But the boy is learning new things each day.

CHAPTER 2

WHAT IS INTELLECTUAL HEALTH?

Intellectual health is about how a person thinks and learns. Intellectually healthy people may do well in school. But this type of health is about more than knowing a lot or getting good grades. Instead, it's about being a person who is always learning and growing. It involves curiosity, critical thinking, and creativity.

Intellectually healthy people often share what they learn with others.

Curiosity is the desire to learn. Curious people seek out new ideas and experiences. They ask questions. They are open to trying new things and meeting new people. These new connections help them find even more interests and ideas.

Intellectually healthy people also think critically. Instead of believing everything they hear, critical thinkers **evaluate** ideas. They consider the **implications**. And they ask questions such as "How?" and "Why?" These steps help people know when information is untrustworthy.

Critical thinking isn't always negative. It also helps people **interact** with new ideas. Instead of getting scared or

Books and music can help people explore different ways of experiencing the world.

shutting down, people can test out new views. And by doing this, they can learn and grow.

Creativity involves putting ideas together to make something new. Making art, playing music, and writing stories all involve creativity. So can solving math or science problems. When people are creative, they use many parts of the brain

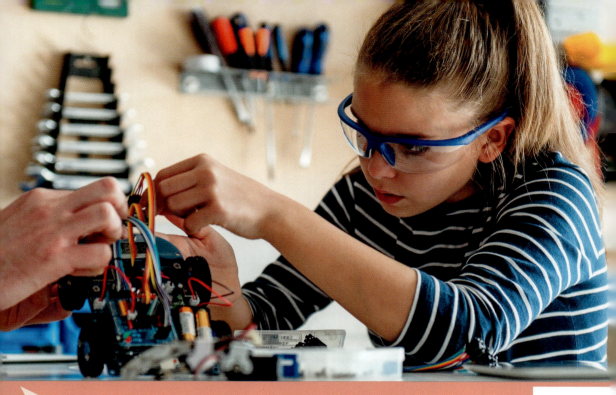

Many science projects involve building or inventing things. This work takes creativity.

at once. This type of work helps to make the brain better at solving problems.

Many factors affect intellectual health. Some of these things relate to the brain. The brain controls many parts of memory and thinking. When it's not working well, learning new things is harder. A person's environment matters, too. Stress and anxiety make it harder to focus. People are also shaped by their relationships. Having friends and family who like learning can make people more likely to be curious. So can knowing people of different ages, beliefs, and backgrounds.

WAYS TO BOOST BRAIN HEALTH

CONNECTIONS

MIND AND BODY

Physical health is about how a person's body works. But it also impacts a person's intellectual health. To work well, the brain needs energy and **nutrients**. People get these from food. Eating foods that contain healthy fats can give the brain a steady source of energy. Fish, nuts, and seeds are all high in healthy fats.

Protein is important, too. The body uses many types of protein. They help it build new **cells**. They also help it make the chemicals that send messages in the brain. Both are important parts of thinking and learning. Beans, meat, and eggs are all good protein sources.

Nutrients from food go into a person's blood. Then they travel to the brain. Exercise helps this process. It gets a person's blood moving. That helps nutrients reach the brain more quickly.

Most kids need about nine hours of sleep each night.

Getting enough sleep is also important. While a person sleeps, their brain stays active. It removes **toxins**. It stores memories, too. Without good sleep, a person's memory and focus suffer. To help, people can stick to a schedule. They can go to bed and wake up at similar times each day.

CHAPTER 3

DIFFERENT WAYS OF LEARNING

Each person's brain is different. So are their experiences. As a result, learning new things can be harder for certain people. For example, some people feel strong anxiety about making mistakes.

People may also have conditions that affect how they think and learn. Autism is one example. Autism shapes how people

About one in nine US kids has ADHD. Kids with ADHD may need extra help to focus.

see the world and how they interact with others. Dyslexia is another. It makes it hard for people to read. People with these conditions may struggle with certain skills or situations. But that doesn't mean they're not intellectually healthy. Instead, they just have a different way of learning.

IEPs

In some cases, students get an individualized education program (IEP). An IEP helps a student get what they need to learn well at school. A team of experts work together to create it. First, they identify the student's learning needs. Then, they list ways to help meet those needs. For example, a student with Down syndrome may get speech therapy. They practice ways to communicate.

A speech therapist can help people practice pronouncing words.

To find what works for them, kids can talk with teachers or school counselors. These adults can help kids find ways to grow and explore their interests. Many schools have therapists, too. These experts can provide extra help.

CHAPTER 4

GOALS AND QUESTIONS

If you want to develop your intellectual health, there are a few questions you can ask yourself. What do you like learning about? Are there times when you struggle to pay attention? What helps you focus during those times? What makes focusing harder? Are there any new activities you would like to try?

Taking a class can be a great way to try something new.

Each person is different. As a result, their strengths and interests will vary. So will the challenges they face. But everyone can learn and grow.

Setting goals helps. Goals break up big tasks into smaller ones. For example, a person might want to learn to play the piano. To accomplish this, they might set a goal to practice 30 minutes a day. They can set smaller goals, too. For instance, they might try to learn one new song each month. Setting **achievable** goals takes practice. But it helps with many types of learning.

People can also practice critical thinking. For example, when reading

A parent or trusted adult can help set goals or check if information is reliable.

a book, you can ask what the author's motivation is. You can look at where the author gets their information. You can check for sources that seem **biased** or unreliable. These steps help make sure you are getting an accurate

23

Making mistakes can feel bad. But it's a normal part of learning. Building new skills takes practice.

understanding. They may also help you find topics you want to learn more about. As you ask questions, you may become curious to find more details.

Learning new subjects or trying new activities can be scary at first. It's okay to ask for help. Talk with a trusted adult. They can help you come up with a plan. And they can bring in more support if needed. For example, they could help you find a therapist. Therapists can teach ways to process fear or anxiety. They can help people practice trying new things.

GROWTH MINDSET

Sometimes, learning can feel impossible. For example, a boy might fail a math test. Afterward, he might think he can never be good at math. He might want to give up and stop trying. However, many things become easier with practice. The belief that people can change is called a growth mindset. People with this view are less likely to give up.

CHAPTER 5

KEEPING AN OPEN MIND

Intellectually healthy people are lifelong learners. It can feel safer or more comfortable to stick with what you know. But it's healthier and more exciting to continue to grow.

One way people can keep growing is by listening. Does someone have a different opinion than you do? Are they interested

Playing games can help people practice learning and solving problems.

in something you're not? Ask them about it in a friendly way. Try to understand why they think the way they do.

After listening, you can share your ideas. Saying what you think can help other people understand you. It also helps you notice things that you are unsure of or want to know more about.

ECHO CHAMBERS

An echo chamber is a group or space where people all think the same way. Echo chambers can occur in person or online. People in echo chambers share the same views. As they post or talk about these ideas, their beliefs and feelings are reinforced. Over time, they may become less likely to talk to people who think differently.

Getting to know people who hold different views can help people stay curious.

As you talk, you may learn information that changes how you see something. Or you may better understand why you think the way you do. Either way, you are continuing to learn and grow.

FOCUS QUESTIONS

Write your answers on a separate piece of paper.

1. Write a sentence that describes the main ideas of Chapter 2.

2. What is your favorite thing to learn about? What do you like about it?

3. Which condition mainly affects a person's ability to read?
   - **A.** ADHD
   - **B.** autism
   - **C.** dyslexia

4. Why might knowing many types of people help someone be curious?
   - **A.** They could get the same answers from each person.
   - **B.** They could disagree with each person's way of seeing the world.
   - **C.** They could learn about each person's different way of seeing the world.

Answer key on page 32.

GLOSSARY

achievable
Able to be done.

biased
Supporting one idea over another, often unfairly.

cells
Small units that make up the bodies of living things and help those bodies perform tasks.

evaluate
To think carefully about how good or bad something is.

fixate
To get stuck doing something or thinking about something.

implications
The results or wider meanings of an idea.

interact
To look at, listen to, or think about something.

nutrients
Substances that living things need to stay strong and healthy.

pandemic
A disease that spreads quickly around the world.

toxins
Poisonous substances.

TO LEARN MORE

BOOKS

Borgert-Spaniol, Megan. *Think with Art! Activities to Enrich the Mind*. Abdo Publishing, 2023.

Eason, Sarah. *The Brain: An Owner's Guide*. Cheriton Children's Books, 2025.

Owen, Ruth, and Victoria Dobney. *The Human Body: Let's Investigate*. Ruby Tuesday Books, 2025.

NOTE TO EDUCATORS

Visit **www.focusreaders.com** to find lesson plans, activities, links, and other resources related to this title.

INDEX

ADHD, 6
anxiety, 13, 17, 25
autism, 17

brain, 11–12, 14–15, 17

creativity, 9, 11
critical thinking, 9–10, 22
curiosity, 9–10, 13, 24

dyslexia, 18

echo chambers, 28

focusing, 5–6, 13, 15, 21

goals, 22

ideas, 10–11, 28
individualized education program (IEP), 18
interests, 7, 10, 19, 22, 27

listening, 27–28

nutrients, 14

questions, 10, 21, 24

school, 5, 7, 9, 18–19
skills, 6, 18
sleep, 13, 15

therapists, 19, 25